Internet Marketing Secrets Unlocked

**Presented By Mason Ramm (Publisher)
Of www.LittleKnownMoneyMakers.com**

Get FREE Internet Marketing Products, Tools & Resources at: www.giveawayclub.net

Legal Notice/Disclaimer:

There is no guarantee of success, traffic and/or that you will make money, either written or implied. The author /publisher specifically disclaims any personal liability, loss, or risk incurred, as a consequence of acting on, undertaking or relaying any advice or information presented herein.

While all attempts have been made to verify information provided in this publication, neither the author nor the publisher assumes any responsibility for errors, omissions or contradictory interpretation of the subject matter herein.

This publication is not intended to be used as a source of legal or business advice. Please remember that the information contained may be subject to varying state and/or local laws or regulations that may apply to the user's particular practice.

The purchaser or reader of this publication assumes responsibility for the use of these materials and information. Adherence to all applicable laws and regulations, both federal, state, and local, governing professional licensing, business practices, advertising and any other aspects of doing business in the US or any other jurisdiction is the sole responsibility of the purchaser or reader.

The author and publisher of this publication assumes no responsibility or liability whatsoever on behalf of any purchaser or reader of these materials. Any perceived slights of specific people or organizations is unintentional.

Information in this report is provided solely for the user's information and, while thought to be accurate, is provided strictly "as is" and without warranty of any kind, either expressed or implied. We will not be liable to you for any damages, direct or indirect, or lost profits or data arising out of your use of information provided in this report.

Every effort has been made to accurately represent our product and its potential. Please remember that each individuals success depends on his or her background, dedication, desire and motivation. As with any business or money making endeavor or venture, there is no guarantee of success.

Proceeding Beyond This Point Constitutes Your Acceptance Of This Legal Notice/Disclaimer.

Brief Introduction

There are techniques and methods in Internet Marketing that you need to know if you want to make money online. They're also pretty useful if you don't want to get burned or spend money you can't afford to lose.

Like all areas of business, those who are 'in the know' use tricks of the trade that become second nature. You may think you know what these trade secrets are, and maybe you do – in theory – but putting them into practice is a different matter. It's like the difference between learning to speak French at school and living in Paris for five years.

More importantly, it is THE difference between people who make money online and people who don't. Those that earn their living from the Internet automatically – unconsciously – without thinking, incorporate these trade secrets – these 'master keys' into everything they do. Often without realizing that they are the secret to online success.

As a pretty successful marketer I didn't realize many of these secrets myself until I stumbled across them. Yes – I know all the sales pages you read claim to 'stumble across' secrets, but I really genuinely did.

I'd hired a ghostwriter to document the processes I use in certain aspects of my business. I was going to publish and sell my own money-making methods.

As I was editing them to use on my sites I noticed certain techniques were included in EVERY SINGLE ONE of my successful sales pages. Sales pages that I'd built that hadn't made much money were ones that DID NOT CONTAIN these methods. I quickly realized that I really has stumbled on something very exciting.

I experimented and put together a great product, great sales page and did everything I usually did expect for one thing. I left out my trade secrets (even though I didn't realize that's

what they were at the time)

The site…..BOMBED!

I failed.

I'd done everything as I usually would **except for using my tricks of the trade** and my site failed miserably.

So I can only conclude that the tips in this book have been the secret to my success.

Now I don't use all the techniques in this book all the time, but I do use SOME of them all the time. I've not added any padding or fluff in this book – I'm going to take you straight to the meat and bones of what I firmly believe can be a life, and income changing read for you.

You're going to recognize some of these secrets – because you'll have seen them on sales pages before. You might even think that some are old and worn out techniques.

LISTEN CLOSELY – You couldn't be more wrong!

There are certain triggers, pushes and manipulations that vastly increase the amount of sales you will make. These are used on the most successful websites in Internet Marketing.

You won't find them on little sites that don't make any money.

But you will **have** to use them to jump onto the wealth bandwagon…and trust me - you will once you see how hugely successful they can make your business, and (let's be blunt) how much money you can make from them.

Welcome to the inner circle guys…..I'm about to hand you the key to open the secrets of successful Internet Marketing…

MARKETING SECRETS UNLOCKED!

Marketing Secrets Unlocked - Method 1

'Old' is the new 'New'

I'm not sure which side of the fence I sit on in the 'there's nothing new under the sun' argument. It's certainly true in Internet Marketing.

Most products contain information that has been rehashed – a new slant has been put on it and it's been given a catchy title (it's all about catchy titles these days) but although it might be better written and the links to relevant sites are new – the info probably isn't.

Nothing wrong with this.

As a buyer you simply need to realize that you're not likely to find any new information in a big launch. Sure – you might find info that YOU haven't come across before but it's highly unlikely to be new to everyone that reads it. This is true of most things in life – the difference is that in Internet Marketing many things are touted as an 'amazing breakthrough' or 'secrets revealed'.

The information contained could still be very valuable of course, but not new.

And so top marketers have realized that if they want to sell a product they should put a 'new' slant on it.

It works something like this.

Author comes up with a product.

Sells product.

Product gets old.

Product is forgotten about by even those who first bought it.

Then someone gets a hold of it. Could even be the original author.

Knows it's an older product, but decides to "re-vamp" it.

Thus, an old forgotten product that is still useful gets **re-announced** and made re-valuable, as a new product.

In other words, you take a product and give it a make-over. Give it a new e-cover(electronic cover), make a few changes to the interior of the ebook file, and viola! A new, yet old, product emerges that markets well, and can make you tens of thousands of dollars.

It's been rehashed. It's like a divorced man – it's been to the gym, got in trim, had a new haircut, got that broken tooth fixed and now it's ready to be offered again.

It's the same old thing of course, but the packaging, marketing and downright 'fizz' are much more appealing.

Of course, this Marketing Secrets Unlocked works, especially with Private Label Products. In fact, it works BETTER.

Why?

Well, for starters, you can re-word the entire product if you want to. Make sure you give it a catchy new title.

 - Add YOUR name as the author, and slip in all your affiliate links to make the product a "multiple income stream" product.

Okay, so what's a "multiple income stream" money producer?

It's any product that can generate more than ONE source of income.

A one source of income product is one that brings income solely by selling the product.

A multiple stream of income product is one which contains (for example) affiliate links, or links to OTHER products you are selling, so that as well as selling the product itself, you get residual income from the links in the book.

It's an easy process.

First, be sure that you can *legally* make changes to the product you've chosen to market (obviously if you wrote it yourself you can do whatever you want with it).

If you've bought resell or master resell rights which come in pdf format this is NOT a problem. Just add your own bonus and zip it up with the pdf. I do this all the time and it's one of the reasons I look at people as though they've gone mad when they say resell rights are dead.

I LOVE resell rights. You can usually (check the license) add anything you like to the package and pass it along with the resell rights product you bought rights too. Most people who resell it are too lazy to change the package in any way – often not even looking at it – so they happily pass along your affiliate links, freebies, website adverts without realizing it.

Private Label Rights (PLR) are usually best for this though because you can add your own money making links in the actual text of the document.

Unfortunately the current trend is that some people put weird and wonderful restrictions on their PLR products. Make sure you read the licenses that come with the product and if in doubt, go for unrestricted PLR, which means you can do most anything with it.

So (where was I?) – first – make sure you're allowed to change it.

If it's a 'rebrandable' product (this means there are certain things you're allowed to change in the product) put in your affiliate or other product sales page link(s) as directed by the original author/creator of the product. Usually you can insert a link of your choice in the pdf that comes with a rebranding tool.

Whichever way you do it, just make sure that the product you're creating (or rehashing or rewriting or whatever) becomes a multiple income stream product by adding your own links. Otherwise once you've sold it, that's the end of your income from it, and the trick is to earn an ongoing income from every single thing you sell.

When you're creating a new product from an old one the key thing is that you update it as much as possible, make it your own, and giving it a snappy title. That way it's more likely to get resold and passed on, which of course is what you want.

I always think that Internet Marketing trends go round in ten-year cycles. Look for old products – chances are you can pick up the PLR for pennies.

If you don't fancy rewriting them yourself use a ghostwriter or freelancer to do it for you.

Most big sellers have a stash of older products to draw from. Think about it – you'd have had to be involved in IM for 10 years to remember the original launch. I WAS and my memory's not that good. I've successfully resold products from five years ago, after a serious rewriting, and nobody's noticed!

Remember - Old to New products.

Put your stamp on it. Re-title it – redo the graphics – put your links in.

Sell it.

Take this to heart and you'll never be short of products again.

Marketing Secrets Unlocked - Method 2

The "Fear Factor" – scare the life out of them.

Used throughout marketing in general – extremely effective In Internet Marketing.

If you believe you may "miss the boat", to coin a phrase, you're more likely you take immediate ACTION.

Which is why we see LOTS of websites with 'offer ends at midnight' or similar slapped all over the sales page.

That's the point of this one. To Make You **Take Action.**

But, there's more to it than just that. It's how you WORD it that really gets people's blood pumping.

Say for instance that you have written what you believe to be a KILLER sales letter. Then, when you type up your "*call to action*" you say. . .

"Hurry. This Offer Ends Soon!"

But WHEN exactly is "soon"???

Soon is such a broad definition in terms of time it doesn't sound real – or scary enough.

'The British Are Coming!!'

'The British Are Coming Soon!!'

Which prompts the most action?

Soon could be two days from now, or two weeks from now. It's great for marketers to try and keep their "special offer" alive for an undisclosed amount of time (they make more sales).

But really, it hurts them in the long run by not picking a designated date and time. That's why when I sell products with that come with limited rights, or are time limited, I shut them down IMMEDIATELY the deadline passes or the licenses sell out.

Make sure that when you use the "fear factor" you give your customers a deadline. And STICK TO THAT DEADLINE! The fear factor only works if you make a date and then remove your offer when the date is reached.

Yeah, you may miss out on a few sales. But think about it this way, the next time you run a time limited special offer your customers will know they had better take you up on it or miss out forever.

And *telling* my readers that I'll be pulling the offer as soon as the licenses are sold is a great selling point to. I'm just drawing their attention to a particular fact – that it's a limited offer – but MAN does it help sales.

Some copy writers call this fear trigger the 'call to action'. Here's an example:

> "Hurry! This Is An Exploding Offer And Will Self-Destruct On Tuesday 14th At Exactly Midnight."

It's even a good idea to throw in a little javascript counter to really make them sweat ;-).

With one of these they can see the time to when the offer ends counting down in front of their eyes.

Then finish up with something along the lines of. . .

> "If you come back here after the above date, you will NOT be able to take advantage of this offer. You MUST ACT NOW or be locked out forever!"

Of course this is precisely how the "fear factor" is supposed to work. Offer your customers something exciting, put a specific time frame on it (a few days usually works great), give them an unbeatable price for what they are getting, and then rip it away from them like a thief in the night.

This works very well as a fast-cash generator too. Putting a time limit of, for example, a week on the offer makes your reader act within a certain time frame. This means you bank the money within a certain time frame too of course.

This will work when you need to get affiliates on board fast too.

In fact this is one of the best ways to guarantee a successful launch. Make it week long then end it DEAD. The activity you'll see within that week will amaze you.

Marketing Secrets Unlocked - Method 3

Perceived Value.

This is a minefield. Luckily, as marketers it mostly works in our favor.

Would you pay $97 for a book on Amazon?

Perhaps – if it was a huge glossy coffee table edition, or a specialist trade manual related to your work. Most people have a $10 limit for book (real, physical books) in our heads and it's hard to shake that.

But convert that thought to an *ebook* and suddenly we're forking out the best part of $100 for a 30 page electronic publication.

Why?

Because of *perceived value.*

When you sell an ebook the value isn't in the physical thing – it's in the information it contains. **Best of all, the value of information is impossible to quantify**. For a start information is more valuable to some people than others.

It's not to do with size either – if I offered you a 600-page ebook on how to make money from adsense or a 1-page document containing next week's lottery results which would you go for?

But because e-products (which I'm focusing on because it's what most of us deal with online) can't be quantified it means we must put some value on them FOR our customers. This basically means telling them what it's worth (great business eh?)

Now this isn't as hard as you might think because most people involved with IM know that an ebook can sell from any price between $5 and $1000 (usually $997), but the normal range for an ebook is under $100.

There are some things we can do to improve its perceived value. An ebook of 300 pages is usually (but not always) perceived as being worth more than a 20-page ebook. Of course there are exceptions to this – if it's written by someone who's classed as a guru then they can probably charge a little more for it.

But when you're reading down that sales page thinking 'I want to buy this ebook' you already have a rough price in your head. If it comes in between $19 and $47 chances are you're going to buy it. Anything above this range becomes an obstacle and undoes all the work done by the sales page.

In short, the perceived value you give to your book should be the maximum you can get away with without it becoming something that the potential customer has to think about.

In terms of volume you're going to have to get around 25 pages minimum into your ebook. Anything less and it becomes something (you guessed it) that the potential customer had to *think* about.

We don't want them thinking – we want them to be rushed along in a sales whirlwind of emotion.

Some of my best selling ebooks have been between 30 and 40 pages in length. That's because I don't write fluff or padding – hopefully you can see that from reading this.

I could pad my books out to 100 pages and sell them for $97 instead of half that but I don't because I have respect for my customers, and want to provide (no fluff) quality information, but mostly because I know they're (you're) not stupid.

People looking for quality information can spot padding a mile off and it doesn't go down well.

So to improve the perceived value of your product BUT also to ensure it sells, you might want to do the following:

1. Sell it at an 'industry standard' price – up to $49
2. Make it over 30 pages if possible, but don't increase the price based on page value alone until you get over 100 pages.
3. Don't make the pricing or (low) page number something that causes your customer

to stop and think rather than buy.

Being different can be a real selling point when marketing your product but if you're going to do it, make sure your product is flawless.

For example I've sold a four-page report for $37, but it was a list of resources that were almost impossible to find elsewhere, which is why people were more than willing to pay for it.

Also is was basically a four page list of websites, so the perceived value was actually quite high (four pages lists a lot of websites)

Marketing Secrets Unlocked - Method 4

Can You REALLY Make Money From "Making Money"?

Yes.

Those that have it want more.

Those that don't have it want some.

And of course, everyone NEEDS it.

I don't know how many people come online each day trying to find a way of making money, but it's a lot.

 I know I did.

Did you?

Through some luck and a fair bit of hard work I found out how to do it.

And the fact that I am known as a successful Internet Marketer is a valuable commodity. I make money online and therefore I am qualified to teach others how to do the same.

But the problem comes when you don't know who is giving out true information and who's is just plain bogus. The new saying 'fake it 'till you make it' is a very real concept online for many marketers.

Once you've found your online money making method it gets easier – far easier – to make more because you can share with others how to do it.

This is ONE of the biggest Master Keys to earning money online

WRITE ABOUT YOUR OWN MONEY MAKING METHODS AND SELL 'EM!

If you can find a foolproof method of making $50 a day from some technique or strategy than people will pay you FAR more than that to share it with them.

$50 a day?

Surely that's not a big enough 'secret' to sell?

Of course it is, because creating money from a PC and Internet connection is nothing less than *alchemy* to some people – it's like creating gold from lead.

…..and if you can make $50 a day online, you can replicate the process and make MORE.

That's what people are buying when you sell your technique in an ebook – not $50 a day but **potential….they're buying the possibility of becoming rich.**

And all you need to do is undertake your normal $50 a day process, write it down, take screenshots and sell it.

Camtasia or Camstudio (software) now provide the tools you need to make simple vides of your technique to sell. You've probably seen the ones – they show what you're doing 'live' on your PC while you narrate the process.

These are very popular (or we're told they're popular) and some say they'll replace ebooks. Personally I doubt it but they are a great way of putting together a product quickly and effectively.

Should you be afraid of revealing your money making secrets?

No.

Chances are, only a handful of people that buy your guide will ever put the information to ANY use. Sure, they'll read it. Maybe even get excited enough to take a few baby steps towards beginning down their own money-making path. But very few people ever complete this process. You can't fight human nature, which is quite a relief for us marketers!

Some clever marketers even give away their techniques for free, holding just one thing back – the TOOLS needed for the job.

Nothing wrong with this – it's a standard marketing technique.

For example if you write a book about how to make $1,000 a week from your mailing list, and to undertake the process ALL the reader needs is some list-building software.

Guess who's selling the list-building software for $200??

I don't do this.

Not because I'm a nice guy, but because I realize that providing an excellent quality money making method will ensure that the *next* time I decide to reveal one of my secrets it'll sell well because people trust me and know I deliver a decent product.

Which is my final point here. You don't have to limit yourself to selling just ONE "How I Make Money Online" product. Methods change or improve over time. So long as you are still learning new methods you remain qualified to write another information product on the subject.

This is one of the biggest tricks of the trade – I'm giving you the Master Keys to open the Internet Marketing money pit here (*how* many IM clichés can I get into one sentence??)

Once you find a genuine way to make money online, you'll make MORE money selling the method of how to do it than you will using the techniques.

That's also (in my book) pretty much the definition of a guru.

Marketing Secrets Unlocked - Method 5

The Persona Is Quicker Than The Eye

Did you know that many successful Internet Marketers suffer from professional split-personality syndrome?

Ever heard of a guy known only online as "The Rich Jerk"?

I thought you might have. Old and tired jerk now eh?

Fact remains it was one of the most impressive marketing campaigns in Internet Marketing. Perhaps by accident.

You'll probably fall into one of two 'rich jerk' camps. You'll either love him or loathe him. He doesn't care which because either way he wins.

If you love him you've probably bought the book. If you loathe him you probably bought the book to see what all the fuss was about.

And if you DIDN'T buy the book I'll bet you've added to at least one forum thread to give your opinion on this genius/doofus.

You (we) have been royally marketed to by the rich jerk. He was headline news in IM land. He got it SO right and his bank account will tell you the same story.

Since the birth of the "Rich Jerk" many an online marketer has tried to follow suit with their own "jerky" persona.

They're only doing what the gurus say we should do -

And that is, to take what already works for other marketers and improve upon it.

The problems arise when there is no foreseeable way to improve upon what was previously done.

Rich Jerk worked because he was the first. The emotions he sparked ranged from anger to devotion.

People see the same technique coming a MILE off now and won't give it the time of day.

The people who jumped on the bandwagon mostly only managed to make people feel *indifferent* towards them, and that's the kiss of death in marketing. If you're going to innovate then INNOVATE – don't be a follower.

This is SO hard to get right. In fact most people who DO get it right aren't exactly sure why it went right in the first place. It's like throwing mud at a wall to see if any sticks.

If it does, great – if not you're just left with a pile of mud and a dirty wall.

Why is why if you're going to try an innovative method of marketing, you might be better doing it under a pen name, or a 'rich jerk' type name.

Because if it doesn't work you could tarnish your real name (your brand) for good.

Most successful marketers including myself write under more than one name. They don't make it widely known but it happens.

Working from behind your PC screen means that you can be anyone at all. You can develop different personalities for different aspects of your marketing. There's nothing wrong in this.

Famous authors do it.

Gurus do it.

I do it.

If you're trying something unusual or away from your usual brand, think about using another name to do it with.

If John Johnson, writing as Trixie LaMuff delivers first class info that I can use to boost my online business, I don't care which name, or even gender, is correct. It's the content that matters.

As long as you don't do anything criminal or run off with anyone's money, a pen name is certainly an option.

Yes, I do know the true identity of the "Rich Jerk", and it's not hard to do a little research to find it, but that was initially part of the hype – who IS the Rich Jerk?

Pen names – other personas - are common place in many industries. Gambling tipsters use them – rock bands use them to play small gigs – writers obviously too.

It's a personal decision as to whether you're comfortable producing products under different names. But whether you're comfortable with it or not, it's a good thing to be aware than many big Internet Marketers have more than one identity.

It gives you the scope to try out new ideas.

Don't dismiss using different personas because you think there's something morally 'wrong' about it. There isn't.

There is no governing body in IM – no rule book and no referees. Try things out – get crazy – get brave – get drunk – whatever it takes to free up your idea monster.

Pen names give you the chance to be who you want to be. In 100 years this won't be possible.

Marketing Secrets Unlocked - Method 6

IS the gold in the list?
It IS if you use this trick….

If you're serious about Internet Marketing, I'd say you pretty much needed to build a list from day one. It can be done without a mailing list but it makes it bloody hard work.

I've heard all sort of figures bandied about on the actual amounts you should be able to make from your list. I honestly think most of it is complete rubbish made up on the spot by marketers when someone asks them.

However, although I'm pretty sure there's no definite answer to how much you should make from your list, I can't help using the following equation when I assess my own earnings from my list.

I'll say now that this is irrational and not based on any research – however it works as a rule of thumb for me.

Not counting new launches, affiliate earnings or any other sort of income from my websites – PURELY going off mailing s to my list, I always try to earn around $0.50 per person on my list.

Obviously this doesn't mean that everyone on my list sends me a dollar (although that would be nice) it means that on average, with some people buying and some ignoring the emails, I average $1 per person per month.

So with a mailing list of 1,000 I'd expect to take in $500 a month from that one list alone.

THAT'S why you should build a list. Because it doesn't take much effort and it's a great source of ongoing income. If you need money in a hurry too, you can send out a mailing and have $500 in your account in 24-48 hours.

I know of someone who uses his (very large) list to fund purchases rather than use banks or credit. He tells me he bought a $300,000 house from a single mailing to his list. I believe him.

I'm not going to go into how to build a list because it's not what this book is about. You can find plenty of free info on the net about this.

I use [Aweber](http://www.aweber.com) at http://www.aweber.com
to manage my lists. Others use getresponse or stand alone software that can be installed on your own server.

To really earn good profits from your mailing list there is a secret. The secret is...

Have More Than ONE List!

That's it. That's the secret.

Now, if you only have one list you rely on to earn money then you already know what to expect. $1 per subscriber. But, that equation DOUBLES if you have two lists to pull in profits from. Want to triple it? Then have 3 lists. And so on and so forth.

Obviously it's not as simple as that. You could argue that a big list would bring in exactly the same sales as a dozen small lists that equates to the same number of subscribers.

Well yes and no.

If you have a large general list you'll get a percentage of sales sure, but not all the people on your list will want what you're offering at any particular time.

Some will be into Adsense, some into affiliate courses, some into viral marketing and others into (for example) software, so might not want an ebook on self-development.

See what I mean?

They've all opted in to your list to get a freebie (presumably) but what the big boys – THE GURUS do, is realize that to make serious money you need to be more **exact about what your list wants**, so they have multiple lists.

Here's how it works. The have multiple opt in pages each offering a different freebie. One might be on adsense, one on affiliate courses, one on viral marketing etc.

Because the opt-in pages are more specialized they know in much more detail what the subscriber is after. So to the list that opted in to get the free adsense course they'll target mostly adsense and pay per click related products. To the people who opted in for the viral marketing freebie they'll target mostly viral marketing products.

And the end result is they end up with a much higher purchase rate than the 'general' list that most subscribers try to earn from.

Really it's niche marketing via a list rather than a website.

Instead of $1 per subscriber, they might make $7 per subscriber.

And on a 15,000 list that's the difference between $15,000 a month and $105,000 a month.

From the same number of people – just more targeted.

This is possibly THE biggest secret that the gurus want to keep to themselves. I'll bet you've not read about it before. Use it – it's worth 100 times the price of this book.

I'm speaking from experience.

Marketing Secrets Unlocked - Method 7

Your Product Must Have A Story...

Everyone loves a good story.

To make a lot of money online all you need to do is to turn yourself into a master storyteller.

Your product won't do much if it's just another 'how to make money online' product. But if it has a story – for example 'Pregnant Abandoned 19 year old almost lost her home UNTIL she found this amazing money making secret'

Now THAT's a story albeit disguised as a sales page (or is it the other way round?)

It's corny – it's hype – but it still sells.

Well.

People need to empathize with you. They need to find common ground with you, because it makes it easier for them to justify to their 'inner voice' why they should buy your product.

I'm not going into the psychology of it all here, but every person who reads your product sales page is having an inner discussion with themselves. They're looking for the 'catch' in your sales letter but at the same time they're also trying to convince themselves why they should buy it.

Experts will tell you differently of course – they're wrong.

Most experts don't write high conversion sales copy. I do.

My advice is to listen to your emotions the next time you read a good sales page. It's like being a child again, listening to a fairy story. You know that it's not all true – but you *want* to believe and all you need is a good *reason* to believe and you're hooked.

That reason is personal empathy.

All the best sales pages try to 'connect' with you in some way. That's why the rags to riches stories always work – the 'used to be in debt but now earn $100,000 a month' stories work.

 Because you are or have been in a similar position, and you want the same lifestyle as the person in the sales copy. They ARE you, in your imagination.

Try split testing your products. Put a sales page that just focuses on the features and benefits of the product on one site, and the exact same sales page, but with a personal story attached.

Watch which one sells better.

That's why earlier in this book I said that once you've learned to make money online you'll earn far more teaching others how to do it.

Because you can tell (sell?) them YOUR STORY about how you learned to do it.

Gurus use stories to great effect. Read the sales pages of the guru's big launches. Empathy – personal stories – things the reader can *relate* to.

It's a huge selling trick.

Are the stories real………..?

Only the guru knows.

Marketing Secrets Unlocked - Method 8

Bums DO Earn Money. . .Online

Bums.

What is your first thought when you think of this word?

A person living on the streets begging for money?

If you're British you might think about arses.

Well offline either is a pretty good description

However when you think about 'bums' online there's now only one thing it really means – BUM MARKETING.

Marketing "bums" are folks that elect to take the easy way to earning profits online. And here's how the real bum marketers do it...

A Marketing "bum" will either write their own, or rewrite another author's 300-800 word article in several places such as free article directories, or on their own web sites including blogs.

(In case you wondered blogs are a great place to post articles.)

But, *within* the articles, they tuck away a few different money making methods such as

Google Ads, affiliate links, and links to their own select web pages that are designed to sell ONE product at a time (any more than one product and most people get confused and leave the page)

Cleverly - all those little money-making methods are related to the topic discussed inside their article.

So for example an article on viral marketing would include a link to an affiliate product about viral marketing (if you buy it, the bum marketer would get maybe 50%).

The web page links in the article would link to another product on viral marketing – perhaps one actually written by the bum marketer.

The google ads displayed would also link to viral marketing products and the clever bums would also have an opt-in link to a 'free viral marketing newsletter' just in case you didn't want to buy anything instantly so they can mail you later with offers.

What's really cool about Marketing bums is the fact that they do next to nothing besides writing up short little articles and offering them for free to anyone and everyone who wants to read them, and still manage to make pretty good profits.

Here's the Master Key secret –
It's the people who use their articles that do the work for them – they're the ones who spread the articles, and therefore the reputation and LINKS of the bum marketer.

After the money starts to come in they can even outsource the article writing (paying $20 for an article to be written) so they don't actually have to do ANY work themselves. Genius.

So, effectively they earn money from giving away free information. Beyond that, they also build up their reputation as a person of value to others by providing such valuable information for free.

It's a win – win situation and that's exactly why the gurus give out so many free reports.

It's not because they're nice people or want to help you with free info – IT'S BECAUSE THEY MAKE SO MUCH MONEY FROM DOING IT THEY'VE ABSOLUTELY NO DESIRE TO STOP.

Obviously this method isn't "new", but it IS a method that brings positive results to those who use it.

I often wonder how many people just don't realize how powerful this method of making money is. We all pay lip service to bum marketing and how great it is, but who actually uses it?

Well I'll tell you now I do.

Because it brings me tens of thousands of dollars a year.

Of course, everyone will earn a different amount.

Some will earn little. And some will earn a lot. It all depends on the effort you put in.

If you only release, or publish, a handful of articles sprinkled with your money making devices, then you can only expect to see a small return from your efforts.

If you get the process as automated as possible using freelance writers you stand to make a lot of money. A ton of money.

The more bum articles / viral products you have out there, the more money you'll make.

There's more to bum marketing than I can cover here but here's my point.

Gurus DON'T give away freebies because they've 'earned more than enough money and now it's time to give something back'

They're not like that. They may have made enough money but they want more. Much more.

Get hold of every 'free' bit of information issued by the gurus and study it carefully. Then copy the exact same method but use different information.

If they have a report about adsense that links to two websites and an affiliate program, write one about blogging that links to two websites and an affiliate program.

Put your links in the same places as they do – word the links the same. Look at the introduction, the way in which they distribute it, where they give it away for free etc and DO THE SAME with your subject.

It's basically a master class on Bum Marketing provided free of charge for you by the guru.

Use it. Most people just look at the free material, maybe read it and that's that.

FORGET the free material. Look at the <u>method</u>.

Copy it.

It could earn you a LOT of money.

That's the secret they DON'T want to give away for free – without realizing it's exactly what they ARE doing – you just have to know where to look to get it…and now I've just told you.

Marketing Secrets Unlocked - Method 9

Squeeze Page Secrets

Squeeze page – a weird term.

You've probably heard the term a few times and not quite understood what it means.

Me too.

Most of the people who talk about squeeze pages only have a slight grasp of the concept – it's just a term after all.

Here's the important bit – this is what a squeeze page should do, and here's how I think it works best.

1. Set Up A Mailing List Subscription Page And Make It The First, And ONLY Page Your Website Visitors See When Arriving At Your Site – so don't distract them with sales offers or adsense ads or links to other pages. You want visitors to do one of two things (hopefully just one) – either sign up to your list or leave.

2. Offer Some Free Information Of VALUE

3. Get them to give you their email address and name, and verify (double opt in) if necessary.

4. Build Your Mailing List

By doing this you build your list and as discussed earlier, INCREASE Your Chances Of Earning Money Over & Over again.

There's a lot of fuss made about list-building and it **is** important, which is why in my opinion you should have a squeeze page, if not several as discussed earlier, for your different lists.

There are different ways to use squeeze pages, all of which should end with one result – the customer signing up to your list.

Here are a few variations on squeeze pages. . . .as used by gurus and not-so-gurus.

1. Use it as your front, or main website page and only offer a freebie or newsletter. They only get the freebie, or access to your newsletter after they've subscribed. This is simple, useable and people know what it's about – they know what to expect from a set up like this. Suits both parties. I'm a fan.

2. Get them to sign up AFTER they've bought something from you. This in effect means they can only get to the download page after they've paid AND given you their email address and name. I don't like this method – and resent it when I buy something and have to go through this. If you give the option of signing up on the download page then that's fine but you shouldn't bully paying customers.

3. Use it in giveaways. Have a pile of freebies and give them, away in exchange for an opt-in (someone signing up to your list). This includes JV giveaways run by other people. You offer a freebie and get sign-ups in return.

4. Use the squeeze type page to let your visitors 'see' if they "qualify" to be added to your mailing list to get special deals and notifications of upcoming special deals or offers. I think this insults the intelligence of your subscribers. Of course everyone will qualify.

Those are just a few different ways to use the squeeze method. Some good, some bad. ALL are used. There are more ways. One is requesting an opt-in before even being taken to the sales page. That bugs me.

Again I prefer the straightforward method.

The principle is easy if you're honest about it. Offer something of value in return for them subscribing to your list

The hard work is in keeping those subscribers AFTER you get them on your list.

Long and boring books have been written on how best to keep subscribers.

Some would say you mail them every day with an offer – others that you don't mail more than once a month.

I have a rule of thumb that works for me. I look at those lists that I choose to remain on (and there aren't many) and work out why I haven't unsubscribed.

Then I copy the methods.

I'll say again you'll learn FAR more by watching what other marketers do than you ever will buying their products.

Squeeze page building is such a huge deal, and rightly so, there are a plethora of products that were created just for this process. All designed with ONE goal in mind. . . .to help you build a great squeeze page.

I don't think you need anything except a bit of care and attention to build a large, responsive list.

Offer a good service or product for free in return for the visitor trusting you with their email address and name. Remember this is like a marriage – once you've got them signed up you can't afford to take them for granted – you have to offer them quality freebies and content as well as trying to sell them stuff.

It's a fine balance – sign up for some guru lists and you'll quickly learn how to do it (and how to NOT do it).

Your list is worth thousands of dollars to you each and every month – look after it.

Marketing Secrets Unlocked - Method 10

The SEO Myth

I'll put my cards straight out onto the table here guys – I think SEO is a load of crap. What little part of it works is so tenuous (search engines change their rules all the time) that it's not worth doing.

There are far easier ways to get traffic.

This is just my opinion, and understanding of SEO.

Experts out there will tell you different. Try SEO – If it works for you come back and tell me. I'm still waiting to hear from *anyone* to take me up on this challenge yet.

When SEO first started out, it was all about using specific keywords, and an abundance of them, throughout your pages to get you a higher rank in search engine placement.

Now, it seems to be all about using those specific keywords **and adding MORE specific keywords inside your website pages generating "long-tail" search strings.**

Eh?

Yeah. It is a bit confusing. So let's start by explaining what, exactly, SEO is.

SEO stands for Search Engine Optimization. It's a method of using keywords and phrases which you put throughout your website pages (including meta tags) to try to get YOUR website pages listed as close to the top of the page in searches that people make on engines such as Google and yahoo as possible.

In essence, SEO is a method where you try and get your website listed on the first page of any search engine search(because when people do internet searches they rarely go past the first page)

The position on the page? If you're inside the top 5 or 6, you're doing pretty well.

But, if you're in the top 3, well, you're doing extremely well.

And being inside the top 3, or even striving to be number one, is the main goal of SEO.

So, the "myth" is, if you got yourself at the number one position of the search engines, then you would most definitely increase your traffic, thereby increasing your profit margins.

What IS true is that if you were ranked number one, you MIGHT see an increase in the amount of traffic, or visitors, to your website.

What is MYTH is that just because you would get those visitors you would earn more money.

Think about it rationally – you could have a thousand visitors a day but if your web page isn't doing its job properly, you're not going to make much more money.

Getting people to your website is only a small portion of having a successful, money making website.

There are other factors at play when trying to earn money online. SEO is only one of those. The fact remains, you could be getting thousands of visitors a day and not selling a thing.

Your website could have top ranking and be the crappiest website in the whole history of crap websites. You won't sell anything.

And of course just to complicate things, the rules of how to optimize your web pages change more frequently than the weather.

Ok.

Now, this is exciting. This is that "trick" part – and it's one of the only ways in which SEO is worth the time and the effort.

You don't really need to know much about SEO to implement this.

Instead of using one keyword over and over again on your pages, and of course, possibly getting kicked out of the search engine ranks for doing it, the trick now is to use "long-tail" keywords.

I hear you saying, "What the hell is a 'long-tail' keyword???".

Hold on, because I'm about to tell you.

A "long-tail" search is one in which a specific phrase (comprised of a few keywords) is used by a searcher to find what he's looking for on a search engine.

Say, for instance, someone was searching for "gravy recipes". That would probably bring back too many results and so the searcher would have to do more searching.

But, if this same person added the word "chicken" or "brown" to the other keywords "gravy recipes", then they would get more specific results presented to them.

So, the phrase "chicken gravy recipes" is considered a "long-tail" search phrase.

What's powerful about "long-tail" search phrases peppered throughout your web pages is that they will naturally rank higher in the search engines.

Naturally?

Yes. Meaning you won't have to do any work to get your pages closer to the top bracket. It will do it all by itself without any extra effort from you!

The search engine does the SEO for you.

So, maybe it's time you went back and tried slipping in a few extra specific keywords to give you that "long-tail" search string and boost your rank.

Be specific about what your website sells or does and you'll naturally climb up the rankings. How it works is beyond me but it works.

So if you have a site about blogging, you could be on page 59 of the 34.7 million results that a search for 'blogging' produces.

And chances are that the person searching isn't interested in your site because it about 'blogging techniques for dolphin chefs'

But if you use the phrase 'blogging techniques for dolphin chefs' which is quite specific, you could well end up at position 1 for this particular search.

And just because it's specific (a niche even) doesn't mean that only a few people will be interested. You might be able to sell your book about blogging techniques for dolphin chefs to 1500 people.

And at $27 a go that's not bad.

So if you're going to use SEO use long tail keywords and let the SEO do the work on it's own.

It's easier and more effective that way!

Marketing Secrets Unlocked - Method 11

Cheap sells.

We're often told that the way to make it big in IM is to sell 'high ticket items'

The problem with high ticket items is that they *cost too much.*

And it's near impossible for someone who's just starting out to sell a product costing $997 with any conviction.

I sell a little report that isn't even mine. I bought it with resell rights and it cost me $3. It's a great value, great content item that I sell at $9.

To date it's brought me tens of thousands of dollars in sales because it solves a problem for people. It's targeted solely at people browsing the net looking for a solution to a particular problem that they have there and then.

My site ranks around 5th on the page for this particular search query

(again using long string keywords – keywords that are pretty defined – eg 'remove Trojan daylight 4442 from Windows Vista' rather than just 'remove trojans').

I rank at this position not because I've spent any real time on SEO (in fact I just wrote the sales page to include my 'string' as many times as possible and the search engines naturally picked it up) and I use a very low priced adwords ad too.

The result is that people find my site and are happy to pay $9 to get their problem solved there and then without having to do any further searching. OR they look at the price and think 'I'm not paying $9 when I can find the information I need for free on Google' and go away and search again.

Two hours later if they've not found the info they need they're happy to come back to my site and pay $9 for the luxury of not having to search any more.

If my product cost $997 they simply would not consider buying it. Sure – I might sell one every three months but it certainly wouldn't bring in the amount of money it has done.

OK – this is important. In my opinion, big ticket items are intended for people to buy as they're caught up in the emotion and hype of a new launch.

Rarely do people go back to an item after 6 months and buy it at full price. Either it's been hugely discounted after the launch or it's now free or comes as a bonus in a membership site.

But rarely does an item for $997 – a big guru launch – cost $997 three or six months after it's been launched. The info hasn't changed – so why not wait and pick it up for peanuts after everyone else has lost interest. I sure wouldn't want to be trying to implement a new money making system (which cost me $997) at exactly the same time as 1000 other people who bought it are trying to do the same thing.

It's insanity.

However lower priced items will keep their value and quietly tick away pushing sales into your Paypal account day after day week after week for as long as you look after them.

You may make thirty thousand dollars (probably a lot more if we're being honest) as a guru launching a high ticket item. You certainly won't as a nobody (as most of us are). But start building good information product sites that sell for small prices and you could find that your monthly income exceeds $20,000 with no trouble at all – and what's more it will continue to do so for as long as you want it to.

People are happy to pay $27 for the convenience of having information compiled and laid in front of them in an easy to read convenient format. They aren't willing to pay $997 for it.

Best of all, by using Clickbank or some other affliate system you can have people go out and sell your small priced products for you for 50% of the profit. Get 10 of these products on the go and suddenly you're able to quit your 9-5.

The guru model of doing things is flawed. It either works supremely well (for a very small few) or doesn't work at all. YET this is the model we're all sold, day in day ouy by big marketers.

Why?

Of course it's because they make money by selling us the methods (we discussed this earlier in the book – more money from teaching others how you make money than actually using the methods you sell!) they use.

Instead why not look at WHAT they do – use the rarely revealed tricks in this book and establish a way of earning online. Once you've done that (again using the secret guru methods in this book) you can hop onto the gravy train, quite legitimately.

And of course, with low ticket items, people can handle the 'risk' better. Put $1000 on a credit card and buy an Internet Marketing course – you'll know the REAL meaning of the phrase 'my heart was pounding'

$27 is expendable. $997 isn't.

Think about this, most of the "gurus" will tell you to "Work Smarter, Not Harder" to earn your money. Meaning, you need to sell far fewer high ticket items to make the same income as selling low ticket ones.

The ONE factor they do not count on is that most people don't have *that* much to spend.

But, those same people have a LITTLE to spend. Those are the people you are going after.

If they're trying to get into Internet Marketing, they want to spend money on something. I did when I started out. If they can afford $997 it doesn't mean they won't spend $27 on your product. In fact it means they're more likely to, because they don't have the option.

The people who CAN afford $997 may also decide to buy your product (what's $27 after considering a $997 product?) especially if the sales page follows the guidelines we discussed earlier.

And of course the BEST reason. If you manage to sign them up for your list after they've bought you'll have FARRRRRR more subscribers than the one or two or bought the $997 for the same profit.

After all profit of $1994 is only two sales (therefore two subscribers) at $997 per product.

If you make $1994 selling $27 products you could end up with 73 subscribers, all of which you can send offers to time and time again.

Conclusion

There isn't one.

Internet Marketing is a game – an ongoing game. You need to see the funny side of it and not take it too seriously.

If you use the tricks – secrets – whatever you want to call them, in this book then you should have successful product launches, and an ongoing successful business.

The main thing – the BIG info is this:

Stop buying products from other marketers because you want to learn how to make money.

Instead buy products because you want to know – inside out – the methods that these gurus use to SELL the products to other people. You're not interested in how they say they earn money online.

Watch how they DO it not what they SAY they do – there's a big difference.

Once you've done that use these same methods to earn money online yourself. Doesn't have to be great amounts – just a gentle repeatable income.

Then write up the method and sell it.

Congratulations – You're on the money train.

Be honest – provide good information.

Keep the ability to laugh at yourself (Very Important:=).

Hope you enjoyed reading this,

Best regards,
Mason Ramm (Publisher)
www.LittleKnownMoneyMakers.com

PS - Did You Get Your Free Membership Yet?
At: http://www.GiveawayClub.net